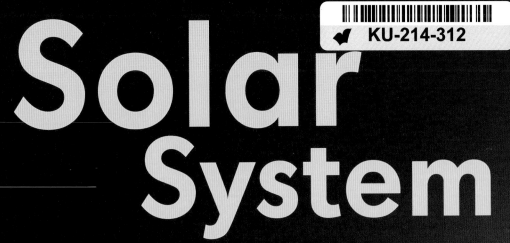

Solar
System

Scholastic Children's Books,
Euston House, 24 Eversholt Street,
London NW1 1DB, UK

A division of Scholastic Ltd
London ~ New York ~ Toronto ~ Sydney ~ Auckland
Mexico City ~ New Delhi ~ Hong Kong

First published in the UK by Scholastic Ltd, 2018

Written by Sue McMillan
© Scholastic Children's Books, 2018
Images used under license from Shutterstock.com

ISBN 978 1407 18894 2

Printed in China

2 4 6 8 10 9 7 5 3 1

Papers used by Scholastic Children's Books are made from wood grown in sustainable forests.

www.scholastic.co.uk

Contents

WHERE IS EARTH?

Have you ever wondered where we are? You know where your house is, and your street and the area around it – the neighbourhood you call home. You probably know which town or city you live in and the name of your country. It is one of many that make up our planet, Earth. But what comes next? Where is Earth?

To find out the answer, we need to take a trip. Imagine that we're on a rocket. We've been blasted high, high in to the sky. Past the clouds and out into space.

In this book we are going to explore Earth's neighbourhood. It is called the Solar System. It is made up of the Sun and eight planets.

HOW DOES IT WORK?

Our Solar System is just a tiny part of space, but it is ENORMOUS!

At the middle of the Solar System is something you see every day – our Sun. Earth is one of eight planets that travel around the Sun. This journey is called an **'orbit'**. A year on each planet is the time it takes to complete one orbit.

There are other things travelling around the Sun, too. There are tiny specks of dust and rocks called **asteroids**. Some asteroids are as small as a tennis ball. Others are bigger than a football pitch!

The Sun

Mercury

Venus

Earth

Mars

Neptune

Uranus

Saturn

Jupiter

Earth's axis

All the planets in the
Solar System spin,
or 'rotate'. A day
on each planet is
the time it takes to
complete one spin.

THE SUN

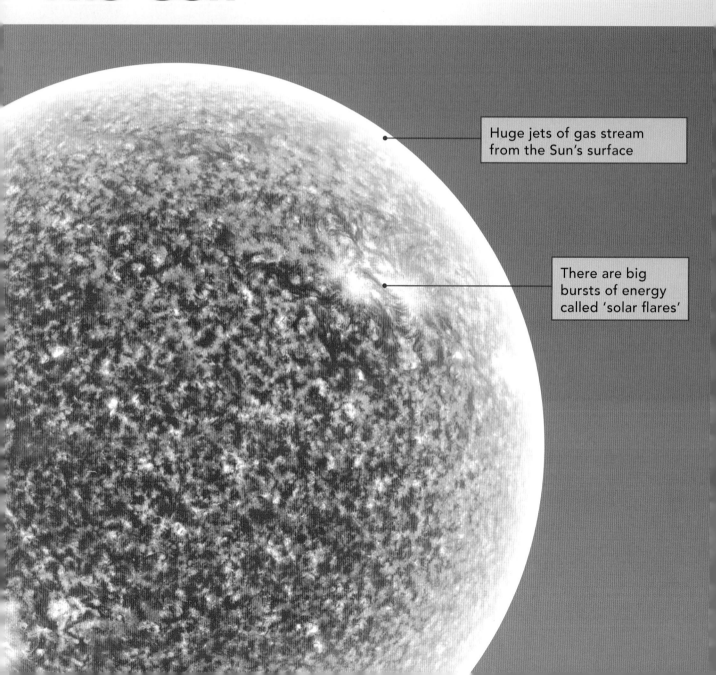

Huge jets of gas stream
from the Sun's surface

There are big
bursts of energy
called 'solar flares'

The Sun

The Sun is a star. It is a ball of fiery gas that gives out the light and heat that we need to live.

It takes around eight minutes for light to reach Earth from the Sun. That's about the same time it takes to cook a hard-boiled egg!

Without the Sun, there would be no daylight. Earth would be a dark, frozen planet, with no oceans, seasons or life. Our Sun is special to us, but out in space there are millions of other stars like it.

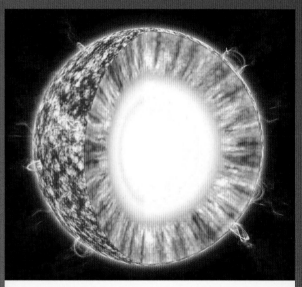

The centre of the Sun is hotter than anything you can think of. The heat and energy it makes travel to the Sun's surface and out into space.

STAY SAFE!

You must **never** look at the Sun directly, or through a telescope or binoculars. It is so bright that it could damage your eyes.

Mercury

Mercury is the closest planet to the Sun. It is the smallest planet in the Solar System.

Mercury is rocky and has huge cliffs. The planet is covered in massive dents called **craters**. They are made when speeding space rocks called '**meteorites**' smash into its surface.

If you were standing on Mercury, the Sun would look three times bigger than it does on Earth. That's because Mercury is much closer to the Sun.

Planet fact file	Mercury
Looks	A grey-brown rocky planet with many craters
Named after	Mercury, the fast messenger of the Roman gods
A day	58 Earth days
A year	88 Earth days
Number of moons	None
Did you know?	In 1631, astronomers Galileo Galilei and Thomas Harriot took a closer look at the planet through a new invention – the telescope.

Venus

Next door to Mercury is Venus. Through a telescope, Venus is orange and looks quite pretty. But you wouldn't want to go there.

The air on Venus would choke you before you'd finished reading this page. The air is also so heavy that it would squash you flat!

Venus is covered in a blanket of clouds. They hold in the Sun's heat, making Venus the hottest planet in the Solar System. The clouds rain a burning liquid called '**acid**'. Venus spins very slowly, so a day is longer than a year. It also spins in the opposite direction to most planets.

Planet fact file	Venus
Looks	An orange, rocky planet covered in thick, choking clouds
Named after	Venus, the Roman goddess of love
A day	243 Earth days
A year	224 Earth days
Number of moons	None
Did you know?	Venus is the second brightest object in the night sky, after the Moon.

EARTH

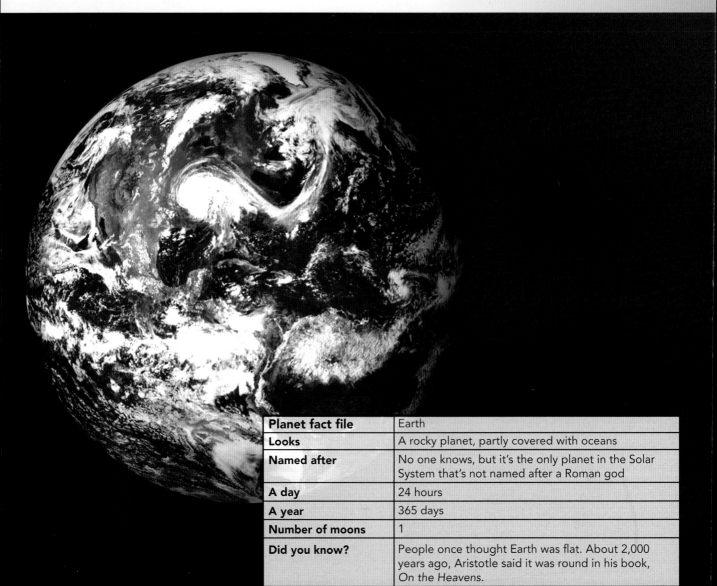

Planet fact file	Earth
Looks	A rocky planet, partly covered with oceans
Named after	No one knows, but it's the only planet in the Solar System that's not named after a Roman god
A day	24 hours
A year	365 days
Number of moons	1
Did you know?	People once thought Earth was flat. About 2,000 years ago, Aristotle said it was round in his book, On the Heavens.

Earth

Our home planet, Earth, is perfect for life. It's not too cold, nor too hot. It has the right mix of everything that humans, plants and animals need to stay alive. We need:

Air – Earth is wrapped in an invisible blanket of gases. This is called the 'atmosphere'. One of the gases in our atmosphere is called 'oxygen', which all living things need.

Heat and light – the Sun warms the planet so that it is the right temperature for plants and animals. It also gives us light – when our side of the planet faces the Sun, it is daytime. When it rotates away from the Sun, it is night-time.

Water – plants and animals also need water to live. Just over half of Earth is covered in water.

The International Space Station (ISS) orbiting Earth

Humans have sent lots of things into space to travel around Earth. These objects are called **'satellites'**. They do all sorts of useful things, like watch the weather, help us to make phone calls and give us directions when we are driving.

The International Space Station (ISS) also orbits Earth. Astronauts visit the ISS to do science experiments. The experiments help us to find out about life in space.

OUR MOON

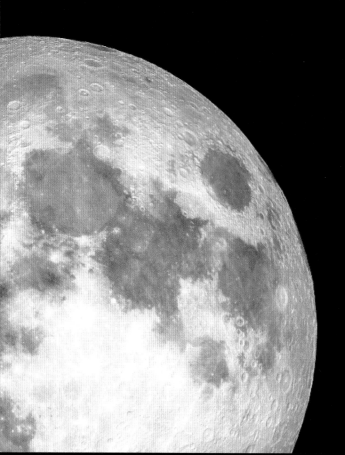

Our Moon

On most clear nights, you can see the Moon. It is the brightest, biggest thing in our night sky. Although it's bright, it's so far away that 30 Earths could fit in the space between us and the Moon.

The Moon has orbited Earth for billions of years. It takes the Moon about 29 days to travel once around Earth.

The Moon is silver-grey in colour and covered in craters, made by space rocks crashing into the surface. These space rocks have left the surface of the Moon, covered in a fine grey dust.

Just a Phase

As the Moon travels around Earth, different amounts of it are lit up by the Sun. This is known as the Moon's phases.

The Moon's Phases

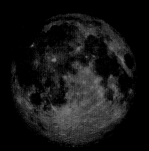

New Moon

Waxing Crescent

First Quarter

Waxing Gibbous

Full Moon

Waning Gibbous

Third Quarter

Waning Crescent

Star Fact

There's **no wind** on the Moon so the Moon's dust doesn't get blown around. It's so still that you can see the Apollo 11 **astronauts' footprints**, many years later.

The Space Race

In the 1950s, the 'space race' began. Two countries, the United States and Russia, wanted to be the first space explorers.

In 1957, Russia sent the world's first satellite, Sputnik, into orbit around Earth. The next year, the United States launched a satellite, Explorer 1.

Russia went one better, sending Luna 2 to the Moon in 1959. In 1961, a Russian cosmonaut called Yuri Gagarin became the first person to orbit Earth in Vostok 1.

Then the United States said they would go to the Moon before the end of the 1960s. They started Project Apollo and, at the end of 1968, Apollo 8 became the first manned spacecraft to orbit the Moon.

A Russian postage stamp with an image of Sputnik, the first human-made satellite

One Giant Leap For Mankind

In 1969, Buzz Aldrin, Neil Armstrong and Michael Collins made history. The astronauts zoomed into space on Apollo 11. They were going to the Moon.

Back on Earth, millions of people tuned in to their televisions to watch the fuzzy black-and-white pictures of Neil Armstrong leaving the spacecraft. As he climbed down he said, "It's one small step for man, one giant leap for mankind."

He was the first human to set foot on the Moon.

After Apollo 11 there were five more Moon missions. The last was in 1972. Astronauts collected rocks and left equipment there to help scientists find out more about the Moon. They also had some fun – one astronaut even played golf!

MARS

★ ★ ★
Star Fact

People used to think that **life** might exist on Mars. There are lots of films and stories about these aliens, called **Martians**, visiting Earth.

Mars

Mars is a little over half the size of Earth. It is drier and colder and has huge dust storms. Like Earth, it has four seasons. Mars is sometimes called the 'red planet' because it is covered in red dust.

There are huge mountains, including Olympus Mons, the biggest mountain in the Solar System. Olympus Mons is three times as tall as Mount Everest, Earth's highest mountain.

Way back in 1965, a spacecraft called Mariner 4 sent back the first photos of the planet as it flew past. So far, humans have not visited Mars, but in 2011 a car-sized space rover called Curiosity landed there. It has been exploring ever since.

Scientists move Curiosity a bit like a remote-controlled car, but much more slowly. It takes more than 15 minutes for the signal to reach Curiosity from Earth and its top speed is 0.14 kilometres per hour. That is slower than a sloth!

Planet fact file	Mars
Looks	A red, rocky planet that's dusty and dry
Named after	Mars, the Roman god of war
A day	24.6 hours
A year	687 Earth days
Number of moons	Two, called Phobos and Deimos
Did you know?	Heat escapes from Mars very quickly. If you were standing on Mars it would feel warm at your feet but freezing cold at your head!

The Asteroid Belt

Next to Mars is the **'asteroid belt'**. There are lots of space rocks here, travelling around the Sun. The biggest is Ceres. It is larger than most asteroids, but too small to be a planet, so scientists call Ceres a 'dwarf planet'.

Star Fact

Jupiter is **so big** that all the other planets in the Solar System would fit inside it!

Planet fact file	Jupiter
Looks	Thick clouds make this freezing-cold planet look like it has stripes
Named after	The king of the Roman gods, Jupiter
A day	10 hours
A year	4,333 Earth days
Number of moons	67
Did you know?	In 1979, Voyager 1 found that Jupiter has three rings, a little like Saturn's.

Jupiter

Jupiter is the biggest planet in the Solar System. It is the first of the four planets called the '**gas giants**', which are mostly made of gases, rather than rock.

Jupiter's gases are red, brown, yellow and white. From space they look like orange-and-white swirls. Jupiter has a red spot. This is a storm that is bigger than Earth, with super-speed winds. The storm has been blowing for hundreds of years.

There are 67 moons orbiting Jupiter. So far, only 53 have names. Ganymede is Jupiter's largest moon. It is also the biggest moon in the Solar System.

Jupiter's Great Red Spot

Saturn

Saturn is the second largest planet in the Solar System. Like Jupiter it is mostly made of gas.

Only four spacecraft have been as far as Saturn. Cassini reached Saturn in 2004. It sent back lots of information about the planet, and its rings and moons.

Saturn has seven rings around its middle. Saturn's rings are made up of millions of pieces of ice and rock. The smallest are like grains of sand, but others are huge!

Planet fact file	Saturn
Looks	This freezing gas giant is pale yellow and has seven rings around its middle
Named after	Saturn, the Roman god of farming
A day	10.7 hours
A year	10,756 Earth days
Number of moons	53 known moons, but there may be as many as 61
Did you know?	Galileo Galilei first spotted Saturn's rings in the 1600s, but he thought they were part of the planet.

Star Fact

Saturn has a lot of **helium**, the gas that is used to fill party balloons.

URANUS AND NEPTUNE

Planet fact file	Uranus
Looks	Blue-green with 13 pale rings around it
Named after	Uranus, the ancient Greek god of the sky
A day	17 hours
A year	30,687 Earth days
Number of moons	27 moons
Did you know?	Uranus is the only planet that spins on its side, like a rolling ball.

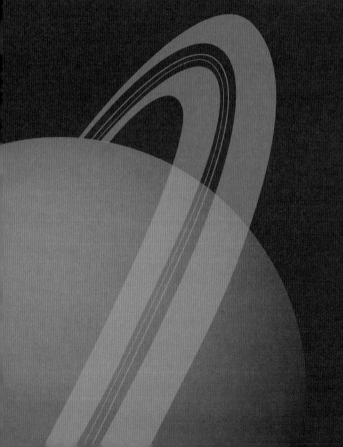

Uranus

Uranus is the seventh planet in the Solar System. It is so far away from Earth that only two spacecraft have ever flown past it.

Uranus is the coldest planet in the Solar System. A spacecraft could not fly down through Uranus's clouds. The freezing cold and pressure would destroy it.

Uranus's rings were first seen around 40 years ago. Scientists thought there were nine. In 2005, photos from the Hubble Space Telescope showed Uranus has 13 rings.

Neptune

Neptune was discovered using maths. In 1846, Joseph le Verrier saw that something was changing Uranus's orbit. He worked out that there must be another planet nearby. He sent his idea to astronomer Johann Galle, who found Neptune almost straight away!

Neptune is so far away from the Sun that one orbit takes 165 Earth years. It took Voyager 2 three years to travel on to Neptune from Uranus. It has sent back lots of information about Neptune and discovered five faint rings circling the planet, along with five moons.

Star Fact

Neptune has done **one orbit** of the Sun since it was found in 1846.

Planet fact file	Neptune
Looks	A bright blue planet with five rings
Named after	Neptune, the Roman god of the sea
A day	16 hours
A year	60,189 Earth days
Number of moons	14
Did you know?	In 1989 Voyager 2 spotted an Earth-sized storm raging on Neptune, called the 'Great Dark Spot'.

THE NEXT SPACE RACE

The Orion spacecraft will take astronauts further into space than we have ever gone before.

Mars Mission

The red planet has been visited by orbiters, landers and rovers.

We have learned lots about living in space thanks to the International Space Station. But the ISS is very close to Earth. Mars is months away. NASA plans to send astronauts to Mars on a spacecraft called Orion. They will find out more about living in space.

If astronauts live on Mars, they will need air to breathe. NASA's new Mars 2020 Rover will test how this could be done.

Many other organizations are also planning Mars missions. Who will win the new space race?

Space Tourism

It may sound far-fetched, but soon it may be possible for anyone to take a trip into space! Perhaps one day, space journeys will be as ordinary as taking a flight from London to New York.

Virgin Galactic will sell short space trips of a few hours so people can see Earth from space. For a short time they will float in the spacecraft, like astronauts on the ISS!

SpaceX has plans for two space tourists to follow Apollo 8's journey around the Moon.

A Virgin Galactic aircraft prototype on display

The Search for Life

Kepler is a space observatory. It was launched in 2009 and has found more than 2,000 planets outside our Solar System.

The James Webb Space Telescope will be launched in Spring 2019. It will find out more about the history of our Universe and continue in the search for life in space.

Star Fact

Dennis Tito was the first person to pay for a **space flight**. In 2001, he spent eight days on the ISS. His trip cost him **twenty million dollars**.

SPACE WORDS

acid – chemicals which are useful, but can be dangerous and cause burns

asteroids – pieces of rock that travel around the Sun, mostly in a belt between Mars and Jupiter

astronaut – a person who has trained to travel in space

astronomer – a scientist who studies stars, planets and moons

cosmonaut – an astronaut who has trained in Russia

crater – a bowl-shaped dent made when a meteorite crashes

dwarf planet – a smaller planet-like object that orbits the Sun

manned – a spacecraft that has humans on board

meteor – a small body in space, which falls to Earth. Sometimes seen as a streak of light, meteors are called 'shooting stars'

orbit – the path an object takes around a star or planet in the same pattern over and over again

satellite – something that orbits a planet. It can be a natural satellite, such as the Moon travelling around Earth, or a human-made satellite that orbits to collect information.

solar flare – a sudden burst of energy from the Sun

spacecraft – a vehicle used for space travel

space probe – an object which is sent into space to send information back to Earth

space rover – a vehicle made to explore places in space, such as Mars and the Moon

telescope – a special tube-like instrument that helps us to see far away things such as planets and stars clearly